The Perfect Tree

Written By : Joseph Durham   Illustrations By : Krystal Kramer

DURHAM
B O O K S
Wild Rose, Wisconsin

Story Copyright © 2024 by Joseph Durham
Illustration Copyright © 2024 by Krystal Kramer

All rights reserved. No part of this book may be reproduced in any form or by any electronic or mechanical means, including information storage and retrieval systems, without permission in writing from the publisher, except by reviewers, who may quote brief passages in a review.

Hardcover ISBN: 979-8-218-35954-6
Library of Congress Control Number: 2024902429

www.durhambooks.com

To my sons and hunting buddies, Tucker, Mitchel and Arthur

In a marsh full of life, under a Wisconsin sky, lived a baby oak tree with wigwams nearby.

So young and so fragile,
how could he have known
just what he'd become
when he was full grown?

Through the wind and the rain and the winters so long,
that little oak would grow so big and strong.

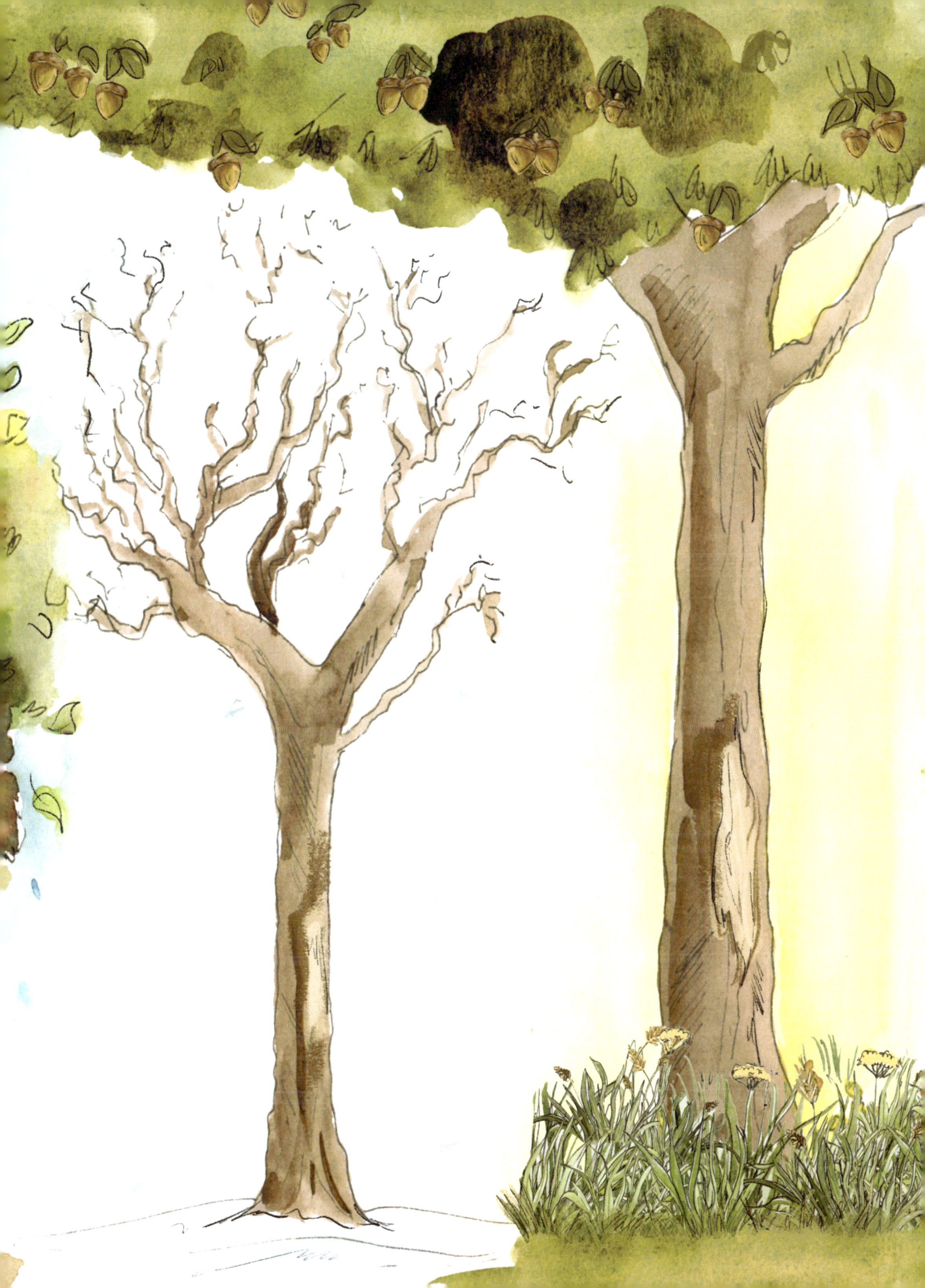

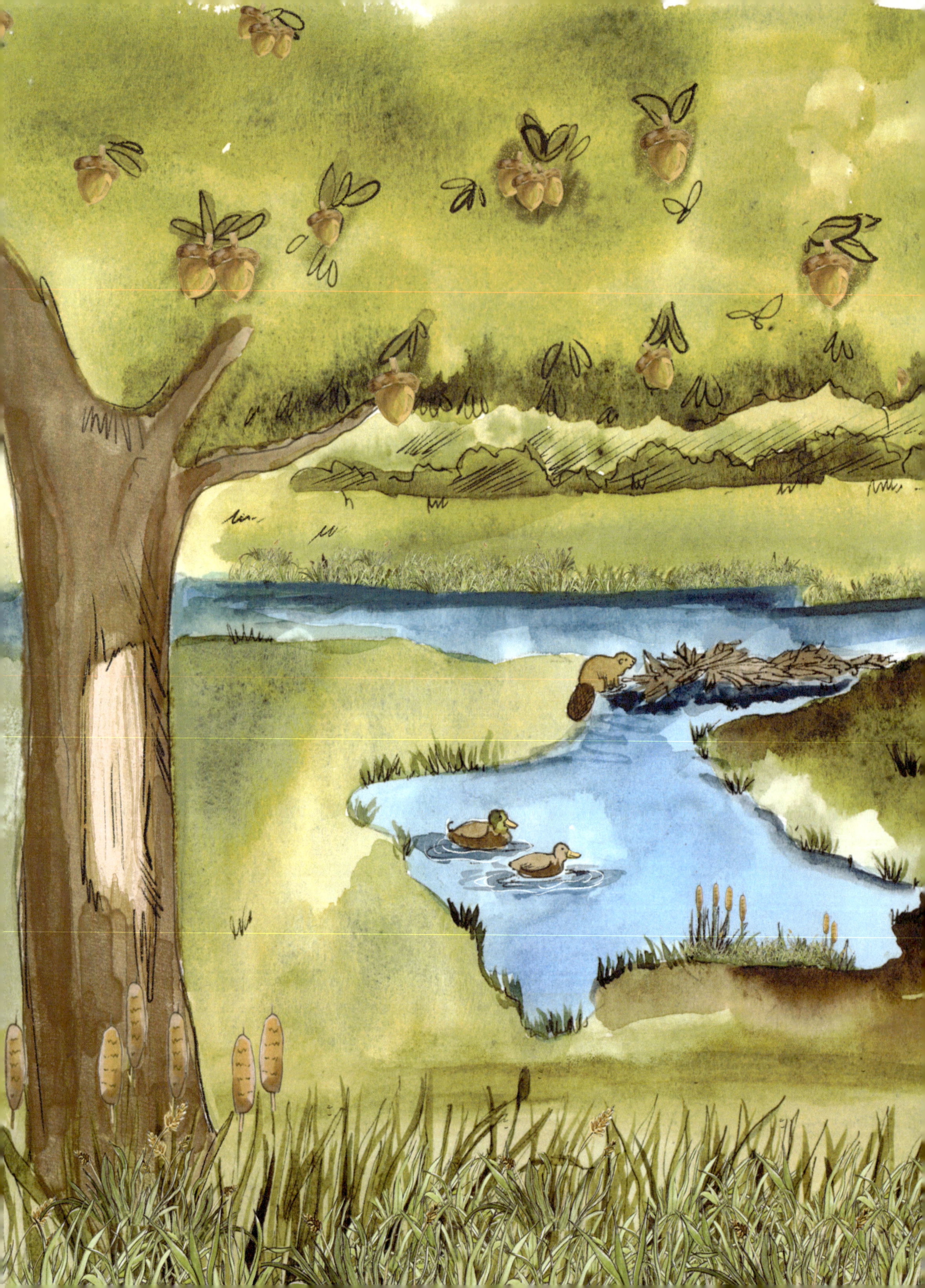

And then one spring morning that young oak couldn't believe. Little Acorns began growing between his branches and leaves.

The oak tree, now tall, would drop those nuts every fall,
for the squirrels, the turkeys, and the whitetail deer most of all.

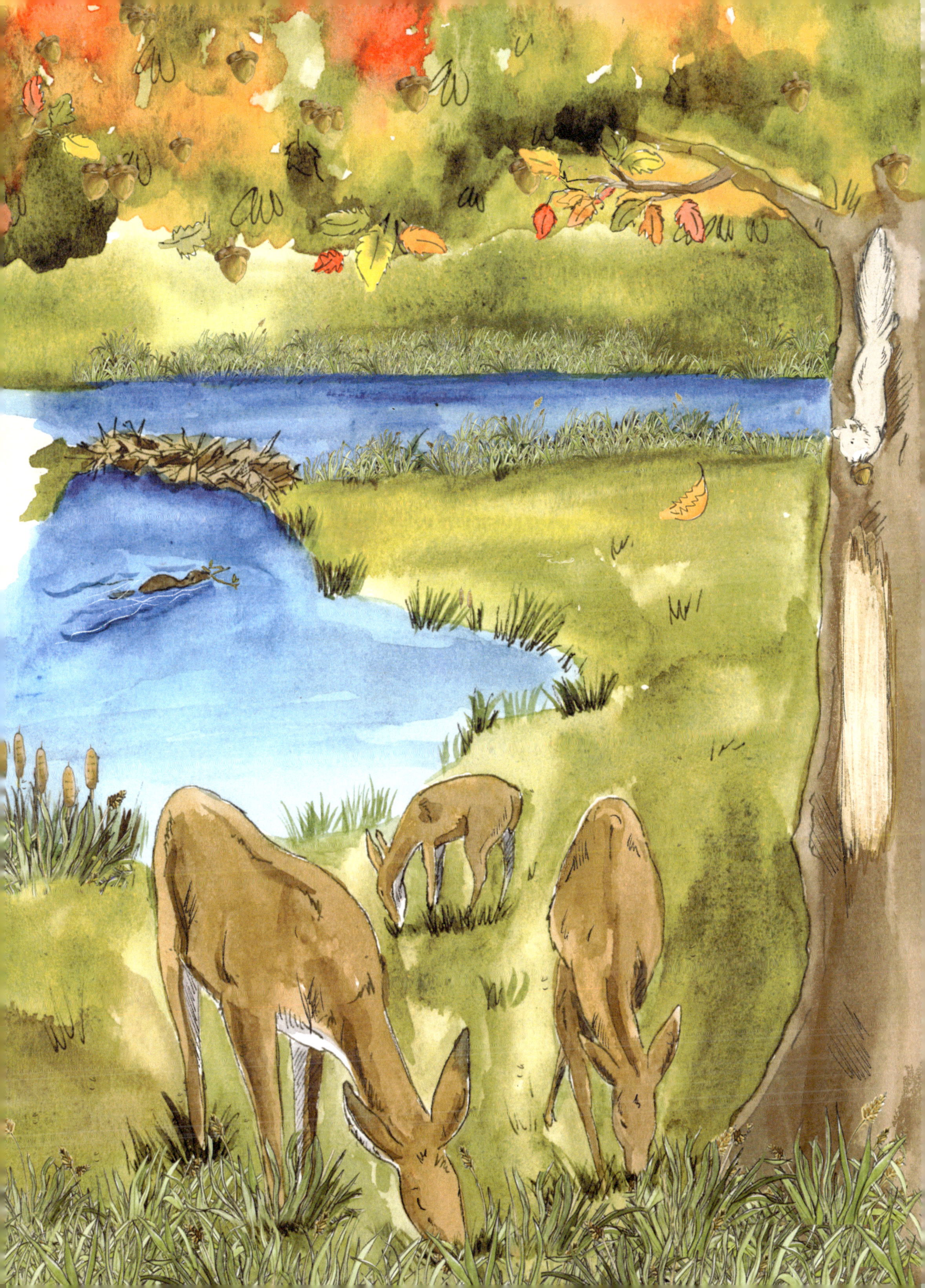

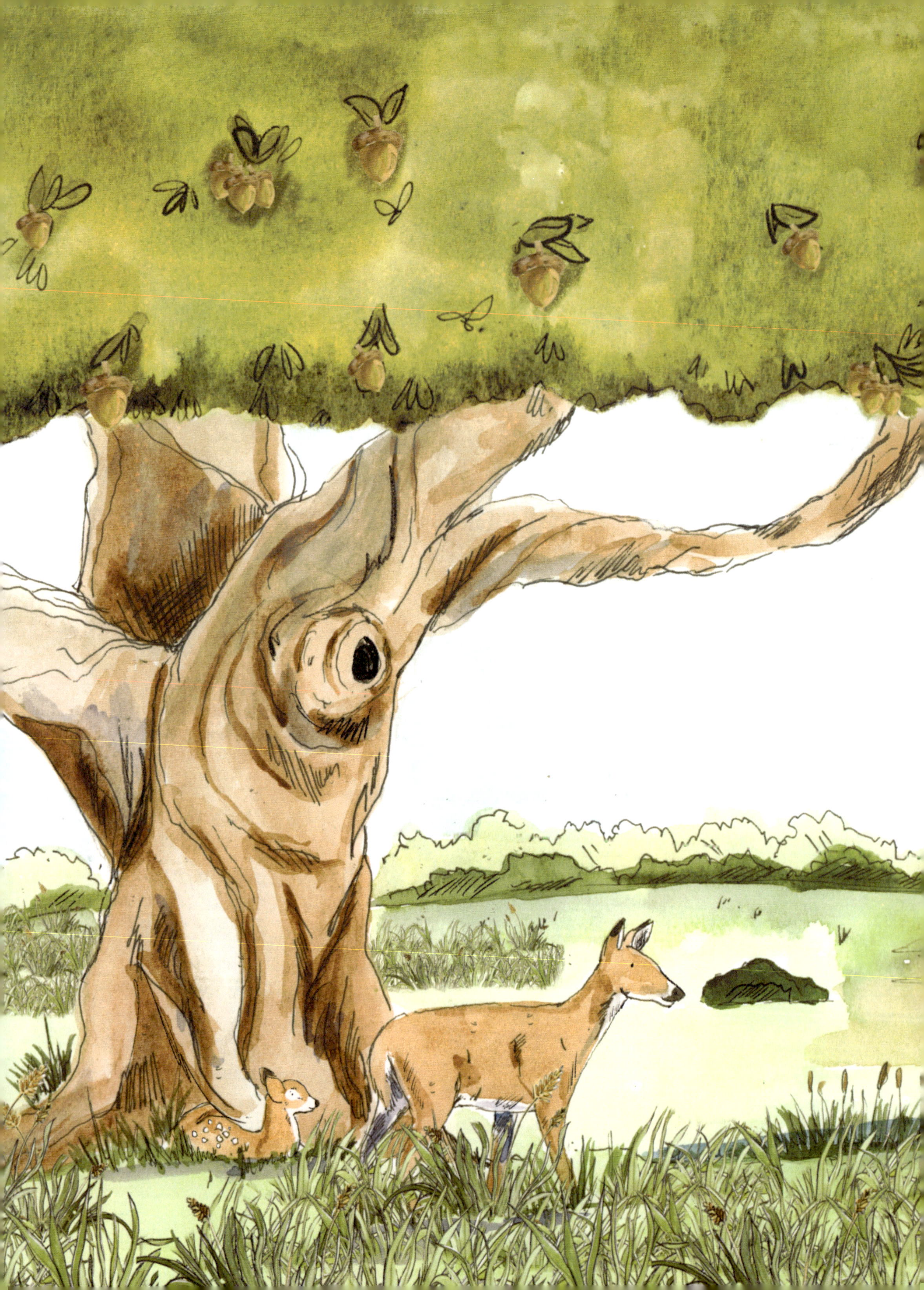

Now the wigwams all gone, the big farming would begin.
That tree kept on growing, the deer kept coming in.

With birds on his branches
And a raccoon den or two
This tree was so happy with the things it could do.

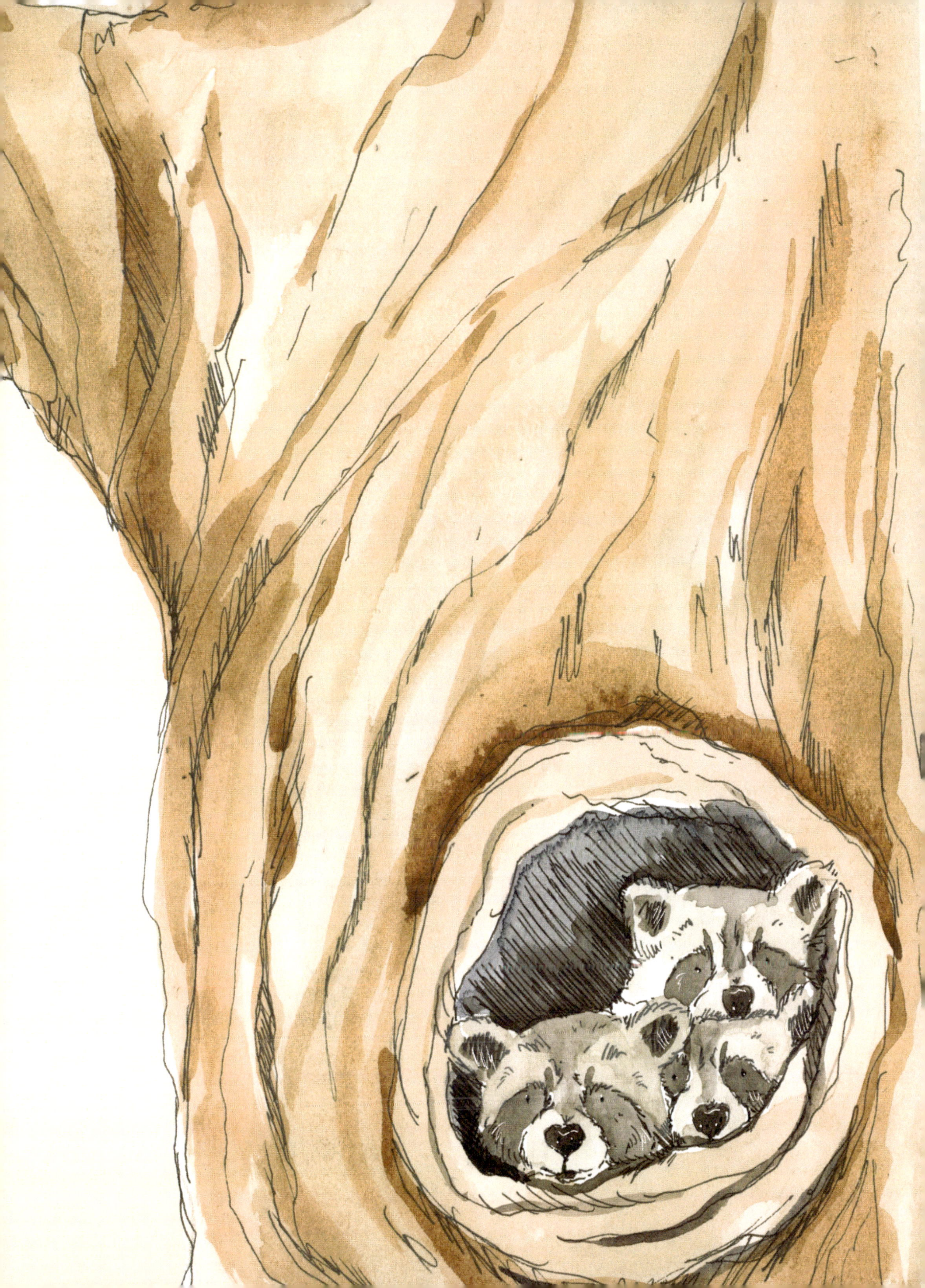

But this tree was special.
With a greater purpose so clear,
God planted this tree to help people hunt deer.

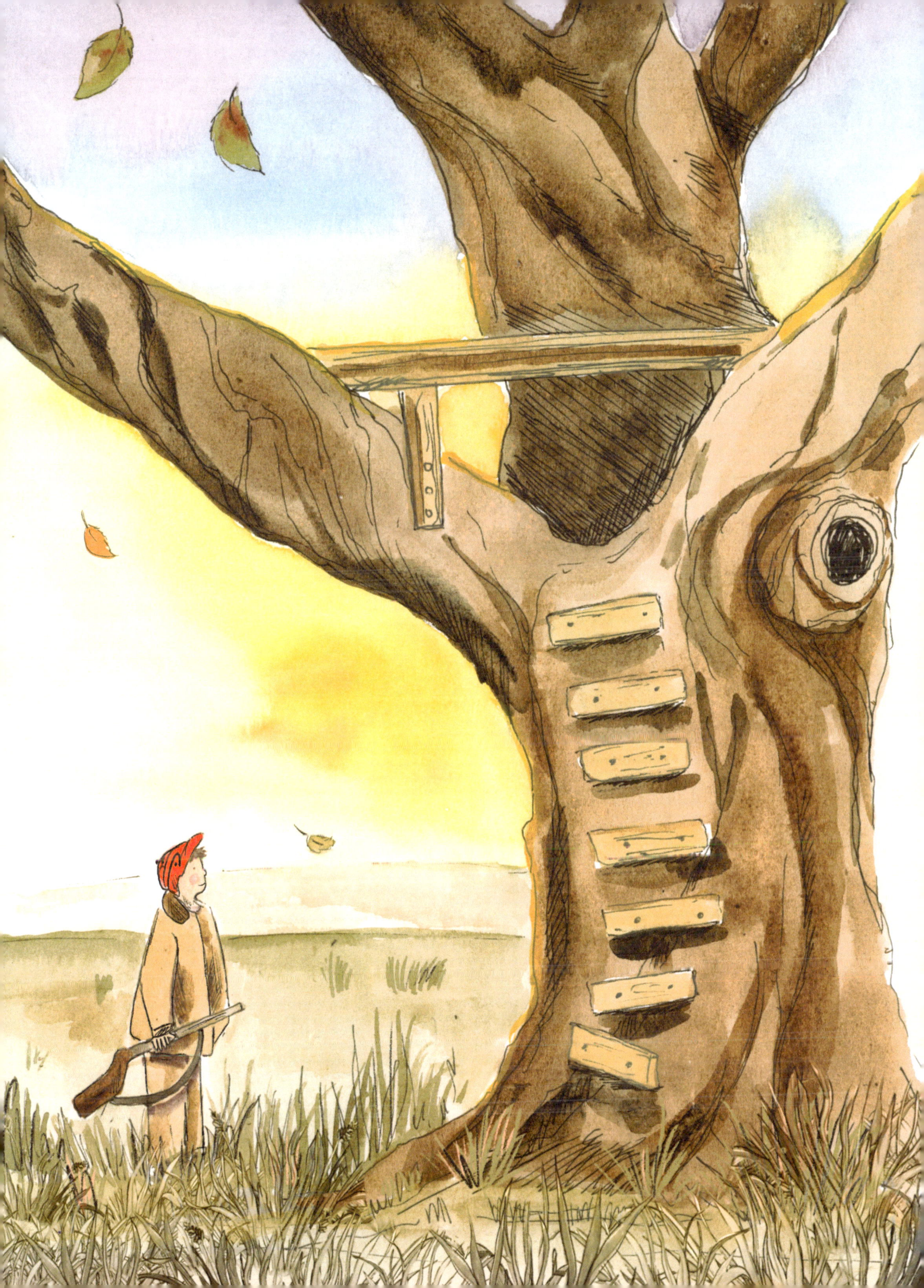

Now it takes a special spot for giant bucks to call home.
A hunter's scouting and hard work could reveal where they roam.

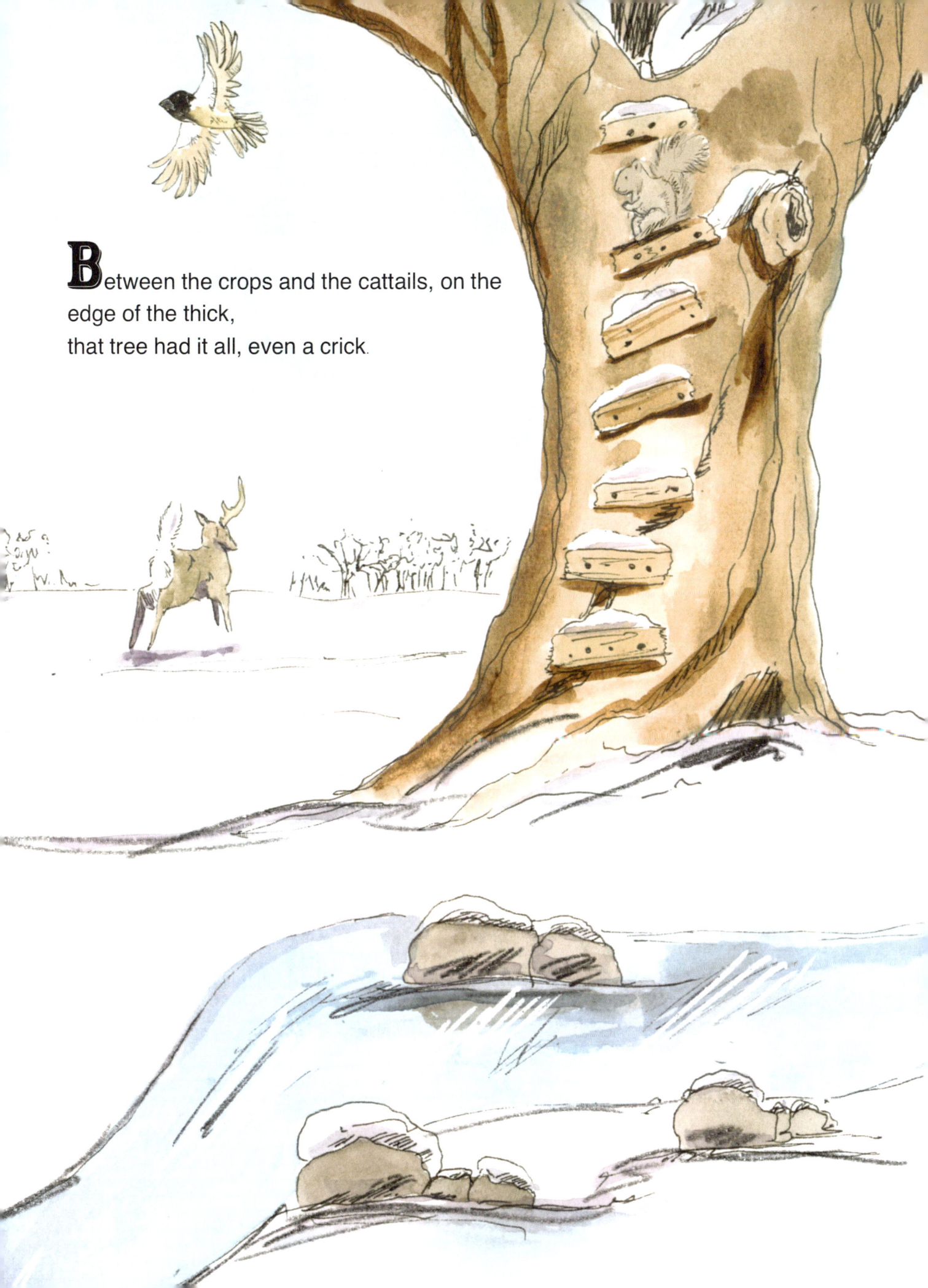

Between the crops and the cattails, on the edge of the thick,
that tree had it all, even a crick.

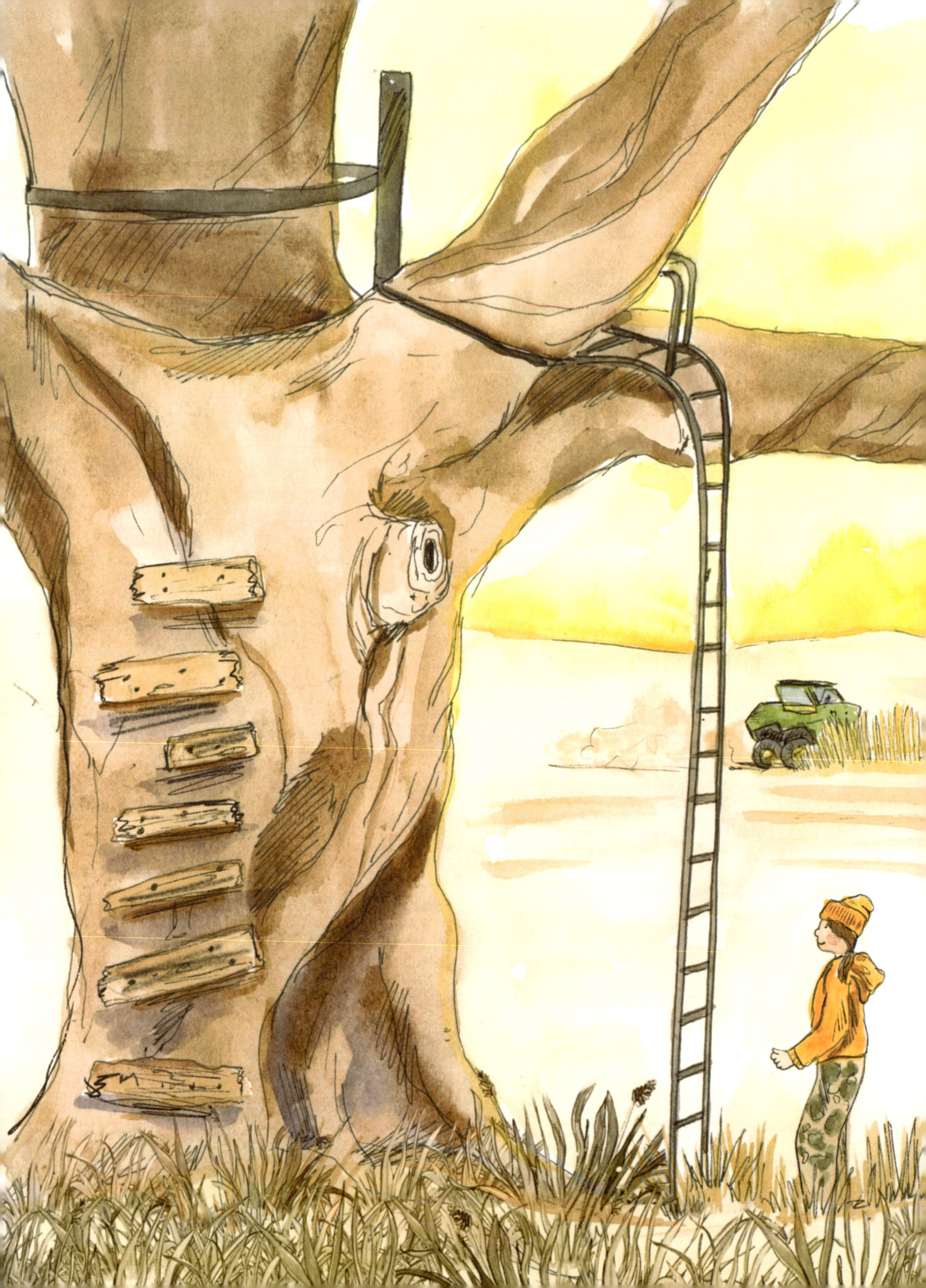

This tree saw many fathers, daughters, and sons climb up its strong branches when deer seasons begun.

Many bucks made people's memories under that tree.
The best hunters knew how perfect this spot could be.

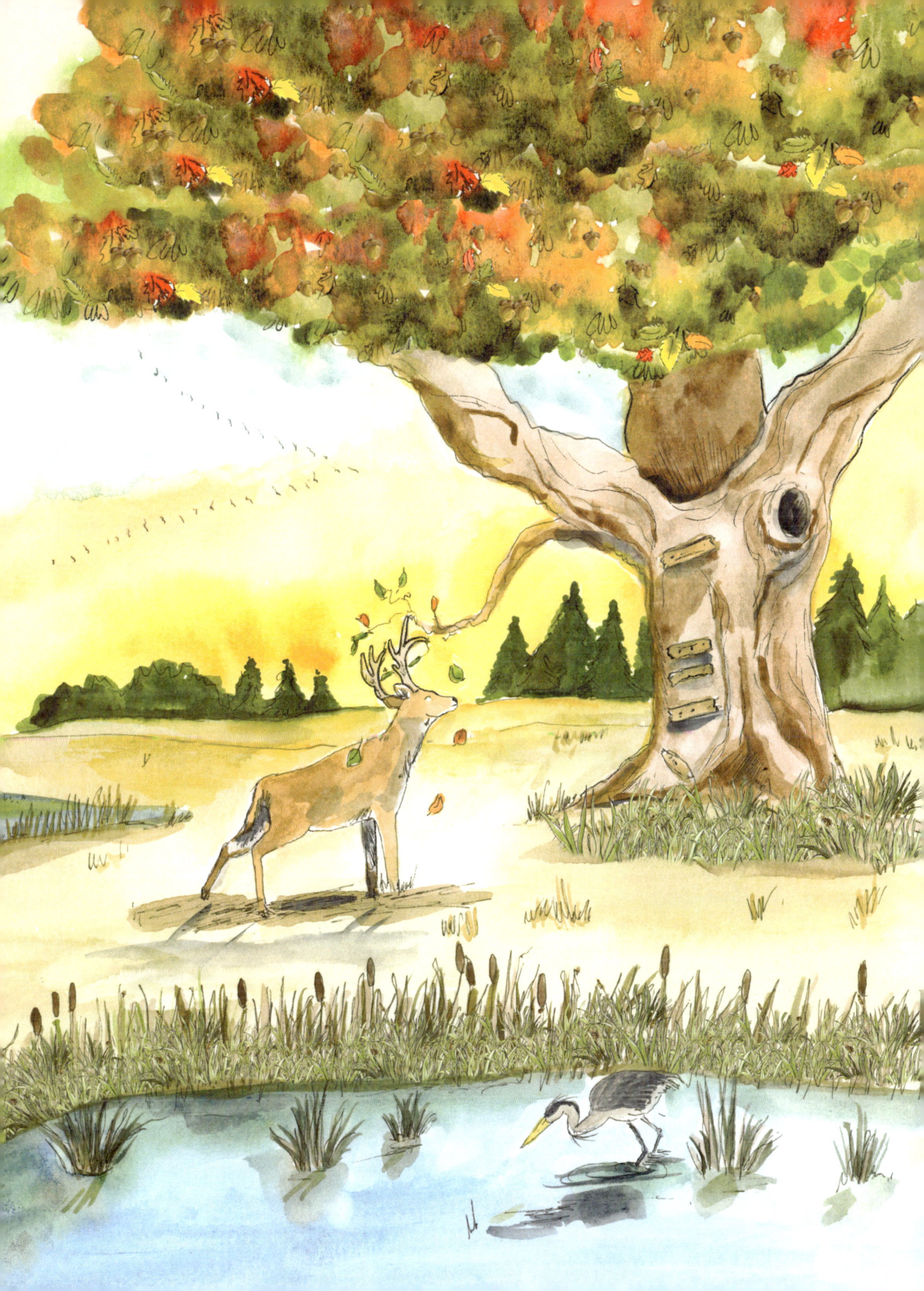

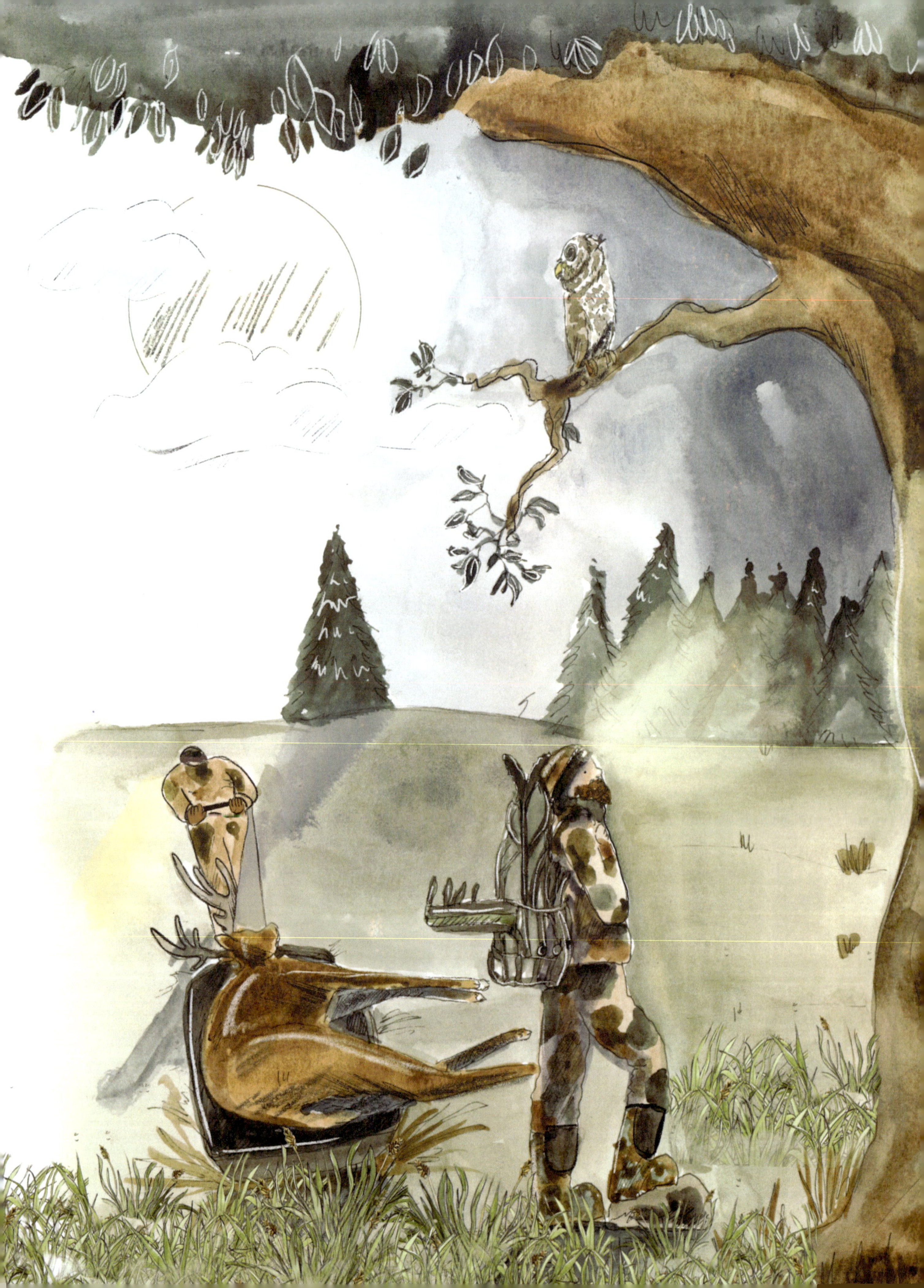

If you're lucky enough to find this tree so grand,
it would be smart to stop and set up your stand.

Sit still and be patient, and with a little luck,
that old oak tree may give you your very own buck.

God bless, and long live the Perfect Tree.

THE END

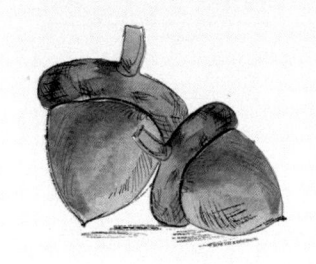

A note from whitetail hunting legend Dan Infalt,

There is nothing more pure or natural than a young person seeking adventure and challenging themselves in nature pursuing game. Hunting has been around as long as there have been prey and predators. To take life teaches you to respect life. To eat meat you took teaches you to respect all animal life, even if it's bought at a store. In the world's fast-paced modern days, young people need an escape. As a hunter you get a front row seat to view Mother Nature in all her glory. You may even start to understand every animal, every bug, and every plant was put on this Earth for a reason and has a purpose. They need to go back to their roots and spend some tree time alone, just them, the animals and God. Alone watching the sunrise over a marsh in November is still the greatest show on Earth.

-Dan

Printed in the USA
CPSIA information can be obtained
at www.ICGtesting.com
LVRC081138111224
798842LV00011B/147